Bishops' Conference of England & Wales

LIVING + SHARING
OUR FAITH

A NATIONAL PROJECT OF CATECHESIS
AND RELIGIOUS EDUCATION

# OUR SCHOOLS AND OUR FAITH

## A pastoral concern and challenge

**JIM GALLAGHER SDB**

Published with the authority of the
Department for Christian Doctrine and Formation

COLLINS

Collins Liturgical Publications
8 Grafton Street, London W1X 3LA

Collins USA
Icehouse One — 401, 151 Union Street
San Francisco, CA 94111-1299

Distributed in Ireland by
Educational Company of Ireland
21 Talbot Street, Dublin 1

Collins Liturgical Australia
Box 316, Blackburn, Victoria 3130

Collins Liturgical New Zealand
PO Box 1, Auckland

ISBN 0 00 599032 7

First published 1988

Nihil obstat     Vincent Nichols *Censor deputatus*
Imprimatur       Ralph Brown *VG*
Westminster      5 February 1988

The Nihil obstat and Imprimatur are a declaration that a book or pamphlet is
considered to be free from doctrinal or moral error. It is not implied that
those who have granted the Nihil obstat and Imprimatur agree with
the contents, opinions or statements expressed.


CREDITS
*Photos*  Carlos Reyes
          except p. 18, Neil Beer
                 p. 13, CIIR
                 pp. 46-47, Collins
*Cartoons* Neil Beer
*Cover design* Neil Beer

Typographical design by Neil Beer
Typeset by Swains (Glasgow) Limited
Printed in Great Britain by Bell and Bain Ltd, Glasgow

# Contents

# Note.

An asterisk, *, in the text, usually occurring after the name of an author or publication, indicates that a reference to the text is given on p. 48, in 'Sources and References'.

On some pages, numbered footnote references are made to specific texts:

*Abbreviations*

AG    *All is Gift*
CS    *The Catholic School*
CSL   *Constitution on the Sacred Liturgy*
CT    *Catechesis in Our Time*
DCE  *Decree on Christian Education*
DCM  *Directory on Children's Masses*
GCD  *The General Catechetical Directory*
GL    *Guidelines*
LCS  *Lay Catholics in School: Witnesses to Faith*
OFS  *Our Faith Story*

It is hoped that these references will prove useful and encourage further study and discussion of some basic principles.

The text of *Our Schools and Our Faith* is the fruit of wide consultation with individuals and groups. The third section, 'Our Schools: Some Distinctive Characteristics' is largely based on the document, 'Evaluating the Distinctive Nature of the Catholic School' which was prepared by a Working Party of the Coordinating Committee for Inservice, Evaluation, Appraisal in Catholic Schools, which is chaired by Bishop Mullins. The discussions of this Working Party have been of considerable value and have contributed a great deal to this book.

4

# Preface

In a time of radical changes in educational theory and practice *Our Schools and Our Faith* is a timely text. It speaks to all who are concerned with the education of children and the young in our schools and colleges: parents, teachers, governors, pupils, priests and parishioners.

In the context of the National Project, *Living and Sharing Our Faith*, this present text addresses the concern to clarify, maintain and develop the distinctive purpose and nature of our Catholic schools. It faces the challenge of doing so in the real world of our schools today: the diversity of religious background, interest and commitment among pupils and staff; the different and changing social and cultural contexts in which our schools exist.

In presenting this concern and challenge, this book should help to make us more aware of the potential of our schools as settings for living and sharing our faith. It should also help us to recognise some inherent limitations of the school in this regard. Its purpose is to encourage us to work at that partnership between parish, home and school which there must be if growth in faith is to be a reality in our schools and if we are to assess realistically their value. As the bishops point out in *The Easter People*, 'the school cannot be expected to do what of its very nature it cannot do alone — produce the fully-committed member of the Church'.

Parents and parishioners cannot expect the school to be wholly responsible for a young person's growth in faith. No more can the spiritual and religious dimension of the Catholic school be left entirely to the RE department and chaplains. All staff, in whatever area of the life of the school they work, are concerned with this, and help create 'an atmosphere permeated with the Gospel spirit of freedom and love' (Vatican II, *Declaration on Christian Education*, 8). This text should be an encouragement to members of staff for them to discover more clearly what is their distinctive role in the school in the light of the Gospel.

*Our Schools and Our Faith* is designed as a working document which will enable interested groups to reflect on, discuss and take whatever action is seen to be appropriate for particular schools and situations. It should prove a useful text for staff in-service days. It is, however, addressed to the wider Catholic community, not just teachers. Our schools are our common concern. They will become increasingly effective and valuable as all of us learn to work together more closely and confidently in the partnership which is their basis and their promise.

✝ David Konstant
Chairman
Department for Christian Doctine and
Formation

# Our Schools Concern and challenge

The Catholic school, both primary and secondary, is of inestimable value to the life of the Church in England and Wales. Whatever new educational priorities may emerge we must neither belittle the contribution which schools have made in the past nor underestimate their potential for the Church now or in the future. . . . The Catholic school should be so inspired by the gospel that it is seen to be a genuine alternative to other forms of schooling. There are many questions which we need to ask about the Catholic school if it is to fulfil its role as a gospel-inspired community.

*Easter People* 134

# Focus and aim of this book

## Focus

a consideration of the potential and limitations of Catholic schools as settings in which we live and share our faith with children and the young in England and Wales today.

## For whom

primarily for GROUPS of Catholics who have a special concern for our schools as settings for living and sharing our Catholic faith tradition: parents, teachers, governors, priests, catechists, parishioners, older pupils. Preferably the groups could have representatives of each of these. With adaptation and more specific questions, the text may be of help in inservice days and staff discussions for teachers and governors who wish to reflect on aspects of the Catholic nature of our schools.

## Aim

to provide a useful working document for these groups, which will encourage and enable them to come together
— to reflect on and discuss issues of concern and challenge;
— to act in ways which will uphold the Catholic character of our schools and meet the particular needs of pupils, staff, families and neighbourhood.

## Themes

1. OUR SCHOOLS: CONCERN AND CHALLENGE
— presents some facts and figures, different situations and the diversity of religious commitment in our schools;
— raises questions concerning the role and duties of the school in relation to faith, religion and individual pupils.

2. OUR SCHOOLS: SOME FACTORS TO BE CONSIDERED
— situates the school in the wider context of the gradual, life-long process of growth in faith, of the partnership of home, parish and school, of today's society;
— raises questions concerning the specific potential and inherent limitations of schools in this process.

3. OUR SCHOOLS: SOME DISTINCTIVE CHARACTERISTICS
— examines some aspects of school life and organisation which are particularly relevant to living and sharing our faith;
— raises questions concerning how these may be more truly inspired by gospel values.

# Some facts and figures

The Catholic community of England and Wales has put enormous effort in terms of finance and personnel into building and maintaining schools for Catholic children. As early as 1852 the bishops at the first synod of Westminster* stated that 'the first necessity is a sufficient provision of education, adequate for the needs of the poor'. Catholics 'should prefer the establishment of good schools to every other work'. Schools, they said, should be built before churches. Prior to the second world war Catholic education was very much a parochial affair. Most parishes in large cities, especially in the north, built their own primary schools. Secondary schools, particularly the grammar schools, were mainly run by the religious orders.

### The dual system

Before 1833 schools were established and funded by voluntary bodies. After that there is a history of gradual but growing financial support from the government. The dual system as we know it dates from 1902. The education act of that year led to the maintenance of county and voluntary schools from rates by local authorities, supplemented by government grants. Other acts, particularly the education act of 1944, more clearly defined the role of voluntary schools within the maintained system.

★ *county schools* are owned and maintained by local authorities who control them subject only to the oversight of the Department of Education and Science.

★ *voluntary schools* are started by groups, generally denominational in character. The control is in the hands of a body of governors and the school is usually held on the trusts of a diocese or religious order. The Church bodies own the schools; the local education authorities maintain them.

### Partnership

Our Catholic schools are closely associated with the national system of education. Maintained Catholic schools are part of the system. The Governors of these schools work in partnership with the local education authority. A capital grant of 85% is provided and the authority is responsible for the maintenance of the school, which includes meeting all its running costs, apart from repairs to the exterior. While there is generous financial assistance, parishes, dioceses and religious orders still provide considerable amounts of money. Complex legal arrangements define the relationship between voluntary bodies and the local authorities.

Local Education Authority

Governing Bodies

| Local Education Authority | Governing Bodies |
|---|---|
| — salaries | — appointment/employment of staff |
| — books, equipment | — admission of pupils |
| — heating, lighting, cleaning | — Catholic character of school |
| — interior repairs | — religious education |
| — meal staff | — exterior repairs |

| CATHOLIC SCHOOLS | TYPES AND NUMBERS | NOS. of PUPILS |
|---|---|---|
| **A.** | | |
| Maintained | 2,417 | 694,065 |
| Independent | 239 | 67,194 |
| Special | 27 | 1,455 |
| Community Homes | 2 | 75 |
| | 2,685 | 762,789 |
| **B.** | | |
| **Maintained Catholic Schools** | | |
| Primary | 1,960 | 385,008 |
| Secondary | 457 | 309,057 |
| 11-16 | 130 | |
| 11-18 | 253 | |
| VIth Form Colleges | 13 | |
| others | 61 | |

FIGURE 1.

FIGURE 2. **PRIMARY/SECONDARY MAINTAINED SCHOOLS per DIOCESE**

Primary school
**Secondary school**

Hexham & Newcastle **27** 146

Lancaster **14** 77

Middlesbrough **16** 52

Leeds **19** 88

Saltford **48** 192

Liverpool **53** 274

Hallam **7** 44

Wrexham **3** 16

Nottingham **18** 67

Shrewsbury **18** 93

Birmingham **41** 218

East Anglia **7** 20

Menevia **3** 13

Cardiff **11** 56

Northampton **11** 42

Brentwood **20** 69

Westminster **50** 169

Clifton **11** 55

Portsmouth **10** 45

Arundel & Brighton **13** 61

Southwark **41** 130

Plymouth **4** 33

(all figures taken from Catholic Education Council January 1987 census returns)

As Catholics we attempt to clarify and develop our understanding of what should be distinguishing features of our schools in England and Wales today.

We need some guiding principles: for example, our schools should be inspired by gospel values and play their specific part in educating our children in our Catholic faith tradition. It is also necessary to take account of the actual people who make up the community of our schools.

**Adaptation to the needs of people and local circumstances is a demand of all pastoral work.** We must try to work out how our particular school can be a setting for living and sharing our faith. We do so in the light of
* Church guidance
* sound educational principles
* the needs of pupils, staff, and locality.

### Some factors

Our schools are involved with pupils, families and communities who have a variety of experiences of life. They are affected by factors which include
* family relationships
* social, cultural, economic conditions
* race
* religious commitment

### Possible changes

Our schools are affected by many changes which take place
* falling roles
* urban development
* population shifts
* unemployment, job prospects
* religious practice and commitment
* multi-cultural, multi-faith society.

~1880~

## PUPIL/TEACHER NUMBERS

Numbers of pupils and teachers in Catholic maintained schools: years with peak numbers compared with 1987 census returns:

**Primary**

| 1974 (peak) | Catholic pupils others | 491,852 8,068 | Catholic teachers others | 17,025 1,855 |
|---|---|---|---|---|
| | | 499,920 | | 18,880 |
| 1987 | Catholic pupils others | 348,112 36,896 | Catholic teachers others | 14,360 1,474 |
| | | 385,008 | | 15,834 |

**Secondary**

| 1980 (peak) | Catholic pupils others | 351,643 11,769 | Catholic teachers others | 14,380 7,396 |
|---|---|---|---|---|
| | | 363,412 | | 21,776 |
| 1987 | Catholic pupils others | 278,451 30,606 | Catholic teachers others | 12,325 7,303 |
| | | 309,057 | | 19,628 |

Number of clergy and religious teaching in maintained schools:

| **Primary** | 1974 | 1,445 | **Secondary** | 1980 | 917 |
|---|---|---|---|---|---|
| | 1987 | 642 | | 1987 | 454 |

## Pilgrimage and journey

Many schools may see their own history of adaptation and change as the story of a pilgrimage and journey of faith. Many have been involved in reorganisation and amalgamation. Many are faced with falling roles. The pupil intake may have changed over the years. We are often faced with the challenge of developing our schools to meet the new needs of pupils and locality which may be very different from what they used to be. Change, like any journey of faith, has its moments of joy and hope as well as its risks, fears, frustration and pain.

---

# QUESTIONS

★ Do you know how much the parish/diocese/religious order pays towards its schools? Where does the money come from?

★ Has your school adapted and changed over the years? In what ways and for what reasons?

★ How would you describe your school in relation to the factors and changes mentioned above? How do these affect the school as a setting for living and sharing our faith?

★ Are you challenged or frustrated by these changes?

-1930-

-1980-

# Creative tensions and balances

We are concerned to justify the existence of our schools on sound pastoral and educational grounds. We wish to uphold their Catholic character in ways which enable us to offer a distinctive yet genuine form of education for all the pupils who attend our schools and which respects the gifts of all members of staff.

This concern poses us with a pastoral and educational challenge : among the pupils and staff in all our schools there can be found a diversity of religious backgrounds and a pluralism of interest in and commitment to our Catholic tradition and way of life.

Among the pupils in our schools, primary and secondary, we will find

- some from families in which both parents are committed Catholics;
- some from homes in which only one parent is Catholic and committed;
- some from nominally Catholic homes in which there is little or no experience of the Catholic faith tradition;
- some from families who belong to other Christian churches or denominations;
- some from families who adhere to other religious faith traditions;
- some from families who adhere to no religious tradition.

Our pupils will gradually over the years manifest their own decision for or against

religious commitment: some from practising Catholic families may give up practice for a variety of reasons; some from families where there is little or no religious practice may express an interest in and commit themselves to the Catholic tradition. Some pupils are dedicated Catholics; some are somewhat apathetic; some may even be hostile and have opted out.

## Tensions

The number of pupils in each of these categories will differ from school to school and from area to area in the country and even in a diocese. Some schools will have very few, if any, pupils from other Christian churches or other faith traditions. All our schools will have a number, sometimes a high proportion, of pupils from homes that are nominally Catholic. We cannot take for granted that there is a fundamental coherence between home, parish and school with regard to the Christian faith. Nor can we organise the religious life of the school and the religious education offered in the school on the assumption that all pupils can be treated as if they were part of a faith community characterised by practising Catholics.

Recent research undertaken by Dr. Leslie Francis* and others suggests that if we run our schools on such an assumption, we may fail to preserve the good will and to enhance the religious development of pupils from less practising homes and from other denominational or faith backgrounds.

## Balances

There are aspects of catechesis and religious education which we must attempt to hold together in a balanced, creative manner. We cannot simply ignore one or other of them:
- to fail to uphold the Catholic character of our schools would abandon the claim for a distinctive form of schooling and do an injustice to our Catholic families and their children;

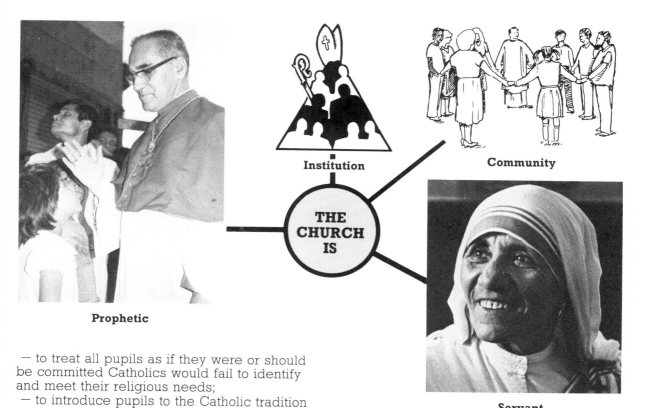

Prophetic

Institution

Community

THE CHURCH IS

Servant

— to treat all pupils as if they were or should be committed Catholics would fail to identify and meet their religious needs;
— to introduce pupils to the Catholic tradition only or to teach little or nothing of other traditions would add to the number of uninformed, prejudiced citizens who find it difficult to respect and live with people who are different.[1]

## Models of Church and school

We often speak of various models of the Church. These highlight various aspects or theological understandings of the Church and emphasise certain pastoral priorities and roles for the Church. A model is useful in so far as it enables us to do this. It is also limited since the reality of Church and school is more complex and nuanced.

## School : *two models*

NURTURING the school is viewed as a Catholic community of faith whose main task is to help Catholic children understand the tradition and participate more fully in the life of the Church.

# QUESTIONS

★ How would you describe the religious background of the pupils in your school?

★ How would you describe the religious interest and commitment of pupils, especially older pupils?

★ What are the reasons for your opinions?

★ How do you react to the tensions and balances outlined above?

★ What models of Church and school do you consider more relevant to your local situation? Why?

SERVING the stress is on the school as a community which meets the human and religious needs of pupils and looks beyond its frontiers to challenge and serve a society which is religiously, racially and culturally diverse.

[1] CS 19, 57, 85.  LCS 12, 41-43.  DCE 9.

B

# Various Duties — Evangelisation, Catechesis, R.E.

The National Project seeks to identify the **various duties** of our schools in regard to the faith and religious development of pupils. Our schools are proper settings for evangelisation, catechesis and religious education. It is necessary, however, that we realise in what circumstances and with which pupils each is more appropriate. Our judgement should be based on sound pastoral and educational criteria, not on presumptions or unrealistic expectations concerning the faith and religious development of pupils.[1]

**Evangelising role** : gospel values inspire and challenge the way we structure and manage our schools, particularly the quality of relationships, and the outlook on life which we seek to live and foster. This is given expression in

**ETHOS**
**PASTORAL CARE**
**BROAD, BALANCED CURRICULUM**

**Catechesis** is addressed to those who have expressed some commitment to the Catholic tradition and way of life. Its aim is to nurture and develop an already existing Christian faith. In the case of children and the young this can take place when they have experience of and are influenced by a Catholic community of faith in home and parish. Their faith is very much dependent on the significant adults in their lives. In time they make a more personal decision.

Catechesis is directed to willing believers — though we recognise different stages, seasons and levels of faith, a place for questioning and searching.

Our schools can provide opportunities for catechesis which enable pupils to deepen their Catholic faith, to live and share it with their peers and to participate more consciously and actively in the life of the Church.

**CHAPLAINCY**
**CELEBRATION**
**LITURGY**
**PRAYER**
**SOCIAL ACTION**
**AWAY DAYS**

**Religious Education** addresses **all pupils in our classrooms** whether they are from committed Catholic homes or not, whether they themselves practise or not, whether they are from other Christian denominations or other faith traditions. Religious education attends to the needs of every pupil who has been admitted to the school.

This does not imply that religious education is a bland form of comparative religion. Some of the aims of religious education in our schools are:

— to help pupils recognise and appreciate the religious and spiritual dimensions of life;

— to lead to a deeper knowledge and understanding of the Catholic and other religious traditions and the ways in which they seek to express the significance of human life;

— to allow space for searching and questioning;

— to challenge pupils to examine their own life stance, to deepen their personal faith commitment and to respect that of others.

Our schools attach great importance to religious education. This is manifest in the provision of adequate time and resources and in the care taken to appoint competent and qualified staff.

Taking account of the diversity of religious background and commitment among pupils in our classrooms, R.E. lessons may lead to different results for different pupils: they can raise awareness of the religious and spiritual in all pupils and also help deepen the faith of some. Teachers cannot simply presume or expect commitment to the Catholic tradition.

In our schools religious education takes place in the context of a community which seeks to live by and foster gospel values and which provides other opportunities for faith sharing and development to those who are open to it.

[1] LCS 28, 42, 56;   OFS pp. 70-75;   GL pp. 12-13;   CS 52.

## RELIGIOUS STUDIES R.E. LESSONS

# QUESTIONS

★ Do you think it is correct to identify the three duties of evangelisation, catechesis and religious education in our schools?

★ Do these distinctions make sense to you? Could you explain them to someone else?

★ In your opinion how can our schools help the faith and religious development of pupils —
  * who are from committed homes and who are themselves committed?
  * who are only nominally Catholic?
  * who are questioning, searching and critical?
  * who are from other denominations and faith backgrounds?

★ How do you view the presence of uncommitted Catholics and pupils of other traditions in our schools?

★ Given the diversity of religious commitment, how would you describe the aims of R.E. lessons?

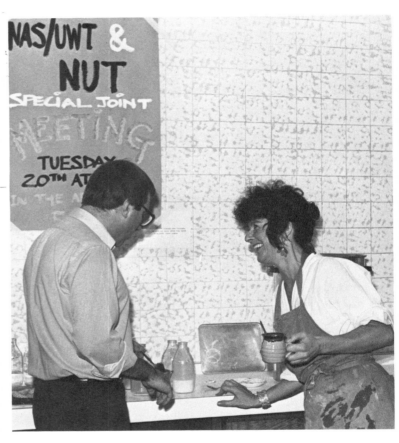

The Church establishes schools because she considers them as a privileged means of promoting the formation of the whole person, since the school is a centre in which a specific concept of the world, of human beings, and of history is developed and conveyed.

*The Catholic School* **8**


We must recognise the limitations of the school. Expectations of the religious education that may be given, and of the growth in the faith of its pupils, must be realistic. The school cannot be expected to do what of its very nature it cannot do alone — produce the fully-committed member of the Church.

*The Easter People* **136**

# Persons and community

One of the prime tasks of our schools is to create an atmosphere of welcome and respect which promotes and makes possible the full personal development of all pupils and members of staff. The quality of personal relationships and an open system of communication are crucial.

### Persons

Education addresses the needs of the whole human person and takes account of the pyschological, social, cultural and emotional aspects of the person as well as the intellectual and cognitive. We must aim at excellence in several spheres without viewing and treating them as separate and unrelated. Each is an essential aspect in a balanced, integrated personal development.

### Community

The school cannot separate itself off from the families of the pupils and the wider community of the neighbourhood. Our schools serve their needs and work with them in mutual respect and collaboration. We should prepare pupils to live in and cope with the world of the late twentieth century and foster a responsible, yet critical, attitude to the society in which they live. We should also encourage pupils to be open to people of different backgrounds, cultures and faiths so that they may be able to live with and learn from the rich diversity which is to be found in Britain today.

The all rounder?

### Common task, different perspectives

Those involved in education have different views on the significance of human life which influence the way they understand and approach the task. Our Catholic schools will have much in common with other schools which seek the full personal development of pupils and staff.[1] At the same time there will be much that is distinctive about the character and environment of our schools. This follows naturally from the faith we profess, from the way we understand and value persons in the light of Jesus Christ.

[1] LCS 1.

# Our Christian perspective

## Our faith

In broad terms faith can be understood as the way we interpret the universe and our place in it. It is our answer to the question 'What does it mean to be alive?' As Catholics we share a common faith : a common perspective on life, a common way of understanding, interpreting and living life.[1] This does not imply that all Catholics think exactly the same. Within the Church there are a variety of theological interpretations.

We profess that in the life, death and resurrection of Jesus we discover the revelation of God's love for us and the true significance of human life.

We acknowledge that every human being is uniquely created by God and destined to share in the life and love of the Father, Son and Spirit; as a consequence, we recognise all human beings as God's family, our brothers and sisters.

We are aware of our sinfulness : we have spoiled God's creation — ourselves and our world — by means of our selfish vested interests which not only affect our individual attitudes but also the corporate expression of these in the ways we structure our society.

Conscious of our failings, we strive, with God's grace, to renew ourselves and transform our world into the Kingdom of God, a kingdom of justice, peace and love.

## Inspiration and challenge

Because of our faith we are impelled to recognise and respect the uniqueness of all individuals and to enable them to become the persons God calls them to be and to help create the world as God intends it to be. We seek to foster a distinctive outlook on life which is rooted in the gospel. Our faith in the Father, Son and Spirit and in the dignity of human life inspires and challenges all we do in our Catholic schools: it should inform the structures, relationships, the aims and objectives we set ourselves and the way we measure success. We assess ourselves in the light of our Christian faith. This is a distinctive mark of our Catholic schools.

## Expressing our faith

Our faith implicitly informs all we say and do. It is also explicitly expressed in our schools in a variety of ways.

These dimensions of our faith will be features of Catholic schools. It is the responsibility of all staff to uphold these ideals. They try to live the values which they wish to foster in the pupils.[2]

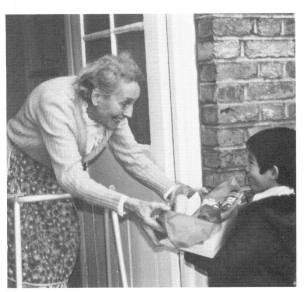

| OUR CHRISTIAN FAITH IS | |
|---|---|
| Experienced | in relationships<br>in the welcome and acceptance of the community<br>in sharing reflection on our experiences |
| Expressed | in scripture<br>in Church doctrine and teaching<br>in the lives of Christians |
| Celebrated | in liturgy and sacrament<br>in ritual and symbol<br>in prayer |
| Lived Out | in service of others<br>in moral responsibility<br>in work for justice<br>in work for peace<br>in respect for all people<br>in dialogue with those of other faith traditions |

Faith and religious development is a gradual process and many influences affect this development. It is a process which includes different stages and seasons which are intricately linked with the stages of our human growth and development. Teachers should take account of these as they introduce pupils to the various dimensions of our Catholic tradition. At different ages pupils will be more ready for and open to certain dimensions.[3]

Account should also be taken of the diversity of religious belief and commitment and different levels of faith among pupils and staff. While our schools seek to live and share our Catholic faith they will respect and have regard for the faith and religious development of all who make up the community of the school.[4]

# QUESTIONS

★ Do you agree with the dimensions of our faith listed above? Would you add or subtract anything?

★ How can our schools provide opportunities for pupils and staff to EXPERIENCE, EXPRESS, CELEBRATE and LIVE OUT our faith?

★ Do you consider some dimensions to be more relevant at certain ages:
* 4-6 year olds?     * 10-12 year olds?
* 15-16 year olds?     * 18 year olds?
Why?

★ How can we make these dimensions features of our schools while respecting the freedom and religious conviction of all staff and pupils? Is this a feature of your school?

[1] GL pp. 18-21;  LCS 28, 42.     [2] CS 32.     [3] GL pp. 22-23.     [4] LCS 28, 42.

# School **One influence among many**

It hardly needs to be said that school is only one influence, though it can be a powerful one, in our development as persons and as Christians. Many people and events influence us over the years. **Our education is not confined to the hours we spend in school.**

### People

Most of our life is still to come after the ages of sixteen or eighteen. We live most of our lives as adults and are deeply affected by the relationships which we form with people in our different spheres of life — family, social, professional and others.

The pre-school years are of particular importance in our personal and religious development: the influence of those who surround and care for us is crucial since it is generally acknowledged that their influence has a lasting effect on us as persons.

During our school years we spend much of our time outside school. Over the years we increase our social contacts and we are influenced by a wider circle of people : family, relatives, friends, our peer group and many others in our society.

Our relationship with people changes and develops. Children are clearly more dependent on parents and other adults than are teenagers. Teenagers still need the help and support of adults but in a different way from children.

### Society

We cannot separate ourselves from the society and environment in which we live. We are influenced and often pressurised, sometimes unconsciously, by the values and attitudes which are constantly put before us in a great variety of ways.

Some of these are positive and beneficial, others are negative and harmful. Some are indifferent and even hostile to the Christian understanding of the significance of human life. Different views and ways of life coexist in our society.

However we may judge these influences, we cannot simply ignore them. We may enhance and complement some; we may lessen the negative effect of others.

We can no longer presume that the pupils in our schools, their families and the teachers

are equally influenced by and committed to the Christian ideal or way of life. From their very early years children absorb values and attitudes which are powerfully communicated through the mass media which are among greatest influences in their lives. Pop culture and peer pressure are especially influential with young people. The Church, for a variety of reasons, may not affect them very much.

## Locality

We are also affected by the social, cultural, economic, religious and political context of our immediate environment of family and locality. Local values, beliefs and attitudes affect the way we relate to people and set our priorities in life.

Our Catholic schools are situated in a variety of places, each with a distinctive social environment. Our children are affected by and ask questions about the people they see around them and the conditions in which they live: rich and poor, employed and unemployed, educated and uneducated, powerful and powerless, those who are included and those who are excluded, men and women with their different roles, black and white with their different life chances.

In the different circumstances in which they live, our pupils have different experiences of our complex society. These are the experiences which they bring to our schools and our classrooms. Reflection on these is an essential aspect of the task of educating them as persons and Christians.[1]

[1] LCS 19, 34, 35;  CS 12, 58;  AG 32-34.

# Influence of school

From Vatican document
*The Catholic School*

★ It is precisely in the Gospel of Christ . . . that the Catholic school finds its definition as it comes to terms with the cultural conditions of our time. (9)

★ School presents an array of values which are actually lived. (32)

. . . creates within the school community an atmosphere permeated with the Gospel spirit of freedom and love. In this setting pupils experience their dignity as persons before they know its definition. (55)

★ Knowledge is not to be considered as a means to material prosperity and success, but as a call to serve and be responsible for others. (56)

★ The school opens itself to others and respects their way of thinking and of living. (57)

★ Motivated by the Christian ideal, the Catholic school is particularly sensitive to the call for a more just society and contributes towards it. It puts these demands into practice in the daily life of the school. (58)

★ First and foremost the Church offers its educational service to the poor or those who are deprived of family help and affection or to those who are far from the faith. (58)

**dignity as persons before they know its definition'**. To do this is to follow the example of Jesus in the way he related to and accepted all people, particularly the poor, the sinners and the outcasts of society. The quality of our relationships with children and the young is the first way we preach the gospel message. It is not simply a matter of teaching Christian values to our pupils, it is a question of presenting **'an array of values which are actually lived'**.

### Structures, attitudes

The way we manage and structure life in our schools already proclaims this message. It is expressed in the ways we show, or fail to show, acceptance of and respect for all in the school community, whatever their ability, religious commitment, social or economic situation, culture or colour. This is the chief way we influence pupils, their families and staff, and also counter-balance some of the more divisive, harmful influences of society.

Teachers are significant adults for children and the young. They are with them at a delicate stage of their development. The teacher's manner, attitude, example and supportive presence probably influence pupils more than any formal teaching.[1]

### Challenges

These quotations from this Vatican document issue demanding challenges to our schools. In a world which is often characterised by depersonalisation and a mass production mentality we must provide **'a setting in which the pupils can experience their**

## Concerned with life

Our schools should be concerned with the real world in which our pupils live. Teachers should be aware of the values and attitudes which are more prevalent and which have the greatest influence on pupils. In this way they can help them reflect on, discuss and question issues which are important to them.

Teachers should be aware of the influences which affect their own values, beliefs and attitudes and the way they assess the situations and experiences of pupils and families. Teachers often come from very different backgrounds from those of their pupils. Our schools must be concerned with the hopes and frustrations of pupils, families and people in the locality which they serve. To fail to do this runs the risk of passing on beliefs and values which may seem irrelevant to their experiences and understanding of life.

[1] LCS 32, 33.

# QUESTIONS

★ In what ways are your pupils influenced by
  * people in their lives? family? others?
  * society generally? the media?
  * local environment?

★ In what ways do particular local needs affect the schools' priorities? Should they affect them?

★ Do you think that the atmosphere of the school and the attitude of teachers have a great influence on pupils? In what ways? Can you remember incidents from your own school days?

★ How do you react to the references from *The Catholic School*? Which seem to you to be particularly relevant and important? Which seem less so? Why?

Children grow and develop in interaction with those with whom they live. From the point of view of Christian faith, it is the quality of the life of the Christians who surround them that has the greatest impact on them.

**Parish and home**

In the Rite of Baptism for Children the focus is on the community which welcomes the child and undertakes to initiate the child into the way of life and beliefs of the community. Most of the rite is addressed to the parents, who are the central figures in the service and undertake to create an atmosphere of love and faith around the child. The community is reminded of its duty to help the parents strengthen their own faith as they take on the responsibility of sharing faith and beliefs with their children. The rite of Confirmation of the young gives similar stress to the role of the community and the parents.

**The task of educating children and the young in our Christian faith cannot be handed over to one or two within the community.** Often parents, priests and others, including teachers and catechists, see this as mainly the task of the Catholic school or of parish catechists.

---

*from Catechesis in Our Time*

★ the parish must be the prime mover and pre-eminent place of catechesis. (67)
★ we cannot make too great an effort to prepare parents to be catechists of their own children. (68)
★ the school provides possibilities for catechesis that are not to be neglected. (69)

---

**Partnership : specific responsibilities**

It is now recognised that while we share this task we each have 'very precise responsiblities'.[1] We have a common goal but we achieve it in specific ways which are more suited to each of the settings of parish,

home and school. We need to consider and clarify these distinct but overlapping roles.[1] The National Project is preparing guidelines for parish and home as settings for living and sharing our faith which will complement these guidelines for schools.

It is easy to talk of partnership. Many Catholics, however, do not at first welcome the emphasis on the responsibilities of family and parish.

HOME · PARISH · SCHOOL

The Partnership

— Some parents would happily leave the work to teachers or catechists.
— Many parents are worried because they are not sure of the ways in which they can educate their children in faith.
— Some priests see it as yet another demand on time, energy and resources.
— Some teachers feel threatened by the stress on parish and home and are less sure of their particular role.
— Other teachers feel liberated from unrealistic expectations.

## Cooperation and sensitivity

Any attempt to create a vital partnership must take account of such fears and hopes. This change of pastoral emphasis cannot just happen; it needs to be worked at with care and sensitivity. It is an educational and

pastoral process which should seek to create, not destroy, community.

This is particularly important on the occasion of preparation for the sacraments. Schools can assist and complement the work of parish and home. They cannot take it over or supplement every deficiency on the part of home and parish.

Teachers, as members of the faith community, have skills which can be of great service in parish-based programmes. These programmes should involve the parents. Adult education methods and approaches should be used and topics should be relevant to their lives as parents and adults. The school may have good facilities which can be used for sessions with children and parents. Circumstances will vary. Much will depend on the working relationships which exist between teachers, priests, parish catechists and parents.

[1] CT 16, 45;   CS 52.

# School as partner

It is clear that as a community we undertake the expense of our schools in order to provide our children with a sound and balanced education within a context which is rooted in and inspired by our Christian vision of life. We recognise the opportunities which the school provides for living and sharing our faith with our children and the young. Historically this is the reason why we built and maintained our schools. It is possible and necessary to preserve that concern while acknowledging the different pastoral and educational needs which we must address today.

Some Catholics would seem to imply that catechesis as education in our Catholic tradition has no place in school, that it belongs properly to the parish and the home. Others seem to suggest that it constitutes the prime purpose of our Catholic schools, whatever the religious background and experiences of the pupils who attend them.

## Possibilities and potential

Our schools can influence the faith and religious development of all our pupils in ways which respect their autonomy as well as their personal and family religious allegiance and commitment. They can do this in a variety of ways which should not be overlooked or neglected:

**Ethos/atmosphere** in which gospel values are lived out and all within the school community experience their dignity as persons.

**Pastoral care** and **curriculum** which in practical ways look to the education of the whole person and of all pupils in the school.

**Chaplaincy work** which complements and adds to other aspects of school life particularly in counselling, links with families and parishes, liturgical celebrations and prayer.

**Voluntary groups** which may concern themselves with prayer, reflection, service and concern for justice.

**Away-days/retreats** which enable staff and pupils to have time and space to reflect prayerfully on issues which concern them and today's world.

**Religious education** which is both inspiring and challenging and concerned with the religious development of all pupils who take part in the lessons.

**Formal and informal links and involvement with families and parishes.**

## Limitations

In the task of educating children and the young in our Catholic faith, schools have to acknowledge certain inherent limitations, for example the variety of religious background and commitment, peer pressure, the compulsory aspect of school and R.E. lessons.

The school cannot produce the fully-committed member of the Church all alone, without the help of parish and home and the free, personal decision of the pupils themselves. A sense of realism as well as optimism and hope are called for if we wish to be faithful both to the Catholic nature of our schools and to the needs of the people with whom we are concerned.

The Vatican document on the Catholic school reminds us that every educational enterprise runs the risk of failure, that there are many formative influences on young people and that results often have to be calculated on a long term basis.

# QUESTIONS

★ What are your likes and dislikes concerning the emphasis on partnership between home, parish and school? Can you appreciate the likes and dislikes of others? Do you know what they are?

★ What do you see as the main functions of home, parish, school in living and sharing faith? in the sacramental preparation of children?

★ Do you see this partnership working in practice? Where? How?

★ Do you agree with the potential of school listed above? Would you add anything?

★ Do you agree that school is also limited in what it can achieve? In what ways?

★ What help and support is needed by parents, governors, teachers, priests, catechists and others to carry out their specific task and to work together? Is any available?

★ In what ways could home-school links be improved?

The concept of faith as a journey is a frequent theme in the writings of the Fathers of the Church and in spiritual writers through the centuries. More recently it has been re-emphasised in Church documents which deal with catechesis as education in Christian faith. The faith journey is a gradual process which continues for the whole of our life.[1]

### Different journeys, one Spirit

While we can recognise certain general characteristics of our personal and faith development, no two people or communities are exactly the same and, as a consequence, each journey is unique. Our personal and community stories are different because they are born out of a variety of experiences of life, such as —

  * family relationships
  * economic and social conditions
  * cultural and racial history
  * religious experience, belief and commitment.

It is important that we appreciate the rich diversity of experiences, personal stories and faith journeys of those we seek to accompany on what, as Christians, we see as our pilgrim journey. It is important, too, that we recognise our own experiences, the strands that make up our personal stories, the stages of our journey and the ways in which these may be different — sometimes very different — from those with whom we work.[2]

To fail to do this is to set ourselves up as teachers only and not acknowledge that we are **learners as well as teachers**. In this way we give practical expression to our belief that the Spirit is at work in different ways in all of us.

### Faith development

There is now available a considerable amount of research and literature on the subject of faith and religious development throughout the whole of our human life-span. Some of the best known works are those of

Fowler, Westerhoff and Moran.* There are different approaches to the subject. Some describe developmental *stages* in the process of growth in faith which we may or may not attain at certain periods of our life. Others speak of *styles* of faith which are characteristic of people at certain ages. When considering the more general features of faith in children and the young during the years in which they are at school it may be useful to speak of the *seasons of faith*.

No analogy is perfect. When we speak of stages of faith, the impression can often be given that it is important to push on and reach the next stage, as if it were not quite right to be at our present stage.

## The seasons of faith

The concept of seasons suggests that each is an essential, important part of the whole: each has its own distinctive features which must be lived through and which should be appreciated and enjoyed. Each season has a basic pattern which we can recognise.

We can, to some extent, chart the weather, though there will always be surprises and the unexpected. No two springs or summers are ever exactly the same. Seasons pass and change and we, too, must pass from infancy, childhood, adolescence through the various stages in adulthood. The seasons come in cycles, so at every age we still live something of summer or autumn. Although we all go through these phases or seasons of human growth, our development as persons and as Christians is unique to each of us. We develop at our own pace and we are influenced by different experiences and events in our lives.

| Young children | are surrounded by the love and faith of the adults who are significant in their lives. They experience and absorb the faith of others. |
|---|---|
| Older children | observe, copy and wish to be part of the faith and religious practice of their family and community, to learn about the tradition take a more active part in celebration. |
| Young people | begin to question the teachings and ways of family and community. They are in search of a personal faith, one they can make their own and which enables them to make sense of themselves and their lives. Although many young people are critical of various aspects of the tradition even to the point of seeming to reject them, they are faced with deeply religious questions and can no longer simply accept the faith and beliefs of others. |

[1] GCD 77-96;   CT 35-45;   GL pp. 22-23.

[2] GL pp. 27-36;   OFS passim.

We accompany children and the young through one or several of these seasons. We should seek to enable them to enjoy the beauty and wonder of each. We are privileged to accompany them and to learn from and with them.[1]

As adults we are in a different season of our journey. We must take care not to judge theirs from our perspective only or to insist that their season of, for example, middle childhood or teens must be the same as we remember ours to have been. There may be many reasons why that cannot be so.

One of the main reasons is, of course, that the world and Church in which they are growing up is different from the one in which we grew up. This and other factors influence their journey in each of the seasons. We must not expect or demand that they experience, understand, celebrate and live their faith in ways which are more suited to our season than to theirs.

## The faith of children and the young

As we accompany children and the young on the journey of faith we must take account of their age, abilities and experience of life. This implies that we have a knowledge and appreciation of the different seasons of early, middle and late childhood, as well as the seasons of the teenage years.

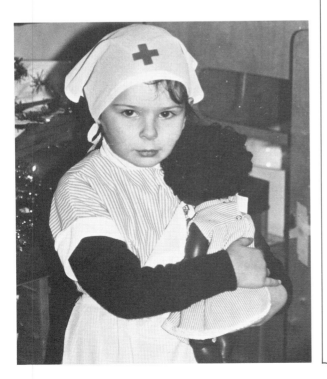

SOME POINTS TO BEAR IN MIND

— ways in which they understand (religious) words and concepts.
— their ability to express themselves in words.
— their ability to read and write.
— other ways in which they express themselves and their feelings.
— the length of time they can concentrate on one thing.
— their ability to recall and remember.
— the people they say they love.
— the ways in which they express love and affection.
— the ways in which they say 'sorry'.
— their main concerns and interests.
— the people and things that make up their world.
— to what extent they are responsible for their own decisions.
— the ways in which they judge right and wrong.
— the people they tend to blame.
— the importance of rules.
— how they react to praise and blame.
— how they express praise and blame.
— the ways in which they accept or question the values of significant adults.
— the ways in which they consider religion as relevant or not to their lives and to issues of importance.
— the ways in which they are willing (or not) to participate in liturgy and other aspects of life in the Church community.
— the opinions they express about the community of faith.[2]

# QUESTIONS

★ Do you accept that growth in faith is a gradual, life-long process? What implications has this for the way you understand faith?

★ Do you like/dislike the analogy of the seasons of faith? Why?

★ Can you recognise seasons in your own faith development?

★ In what ways do you see yourself as a companion with children, the young and others in the journey of faith?

★ In what ways should some of the points mentioned above influence, for example
  * the celebration of eucharist/reconciliation with 8 year olds? with sixth formers? other groups?
  * the way teachers try to help pupils appreciate and understand creation, sin, other doctrines at 5? 13? 18?

★ Do you think parents, priests and others bear these points in mind when they assess what pupils should know and how they practise their faith? Is it important that they should?

[1] LCS 33.   [2] AG pp. 34-35.

The school must be a community whose values are communicated through the interpersonal and sincere relationships of its members and through both individual and corporate adherence to the outlook on life that permeates the school.

*The Catholic School* **32**

It must never be forgotten that the school itself is always in the process of being created, due to the labour brought to fruition by all those who have a role to play in it, and most especially by those who are teachers.

*Lay Catholics in Schools* **78**

# Our Schools In what way distinctive?

Our Catholic schools are, or should be, distinctive because their entire educational policy and approach are inspired by and flow from the vision of life which is enshrined in our faith tradition. Our schools are *not* distinctive *simply* because they timetable more R.E. lessons which concentrate on teaching the Catholic faith, or because they provide opportunities for sacramental celebrations.

Our Catholic faith perspective is not simply an added extra which we teach and offer our pupils; it is integrated into the whole life of our schools and into all aspects of the curriculum; it is conveyed in values and attitudes which are incorporated into the way our schools are structured and managed, into the relationships between the members of staff, and between staff and pupils, into the aims and priorities we set ourselves, and into the procedures by which we evaluate our success. We believe that the Christian vision of life can enable human beings to be more human.[1] We undertake to present it, live it and celebrate it in our schools without in any way imposing it on pupils, staff or families.

## Policy statements and evaluation

It is important that the Prospectus issued by our schools outline the Christian aims and values which underpin our educational endeavours. Governors should give clear guidelines to teachers and parents concerning the Catholic character of our schools. The Prospectus should outline practical objectives which each school seeks to attain in its particular situation in ways which take account of the nature and purpose of the school, as well as the needs of pupils, their families and the locality.

Formal procedures should be established which will enable governors and staff to gauge accurately how far our schools are really achieving what they set out to do. Opportunities should be given to all who make up the school community — staff, governors, parents, pupils — to express opinions about the school and to feel that they are listened to and given serious consideration.

## Appointments and admissions

It is the staff, Catholic or not, 'who will substantially determine whether or not a school realises its aims and accomplishes its objectives'.[2] Those who take up a post in our schools should be in sympathy with, respect and support their distinctive character. This should be outlined in the job description.[3] There will, of course, always be a pluralism of belief and commitment among members of staff. If staff work together to uphold the goals of our schools, this can be a source of enrichment.

The same principle applies to parents who ask to have their children admitted to our schools. Even if they are not themselves committed to the Catholic tradition, they should respect and support the aims of the school and be willing for their children to be part of the school community.

It is the duty of the governors to set out criteria for the appointment of staff and the admission of pupils. At the same time governors and staff must fulfil their duty to further the human and religious development of all pupils who have been accepted into the school community.

## QUESTIONS

★ Do you agree that the Catholic dimension is not something added on to the other aspects of school life but that it permeates everything? Practically, what does that mean?

★ What is the policy statement of your school? Does it set out practical objectives? Do you agree with them?

★ What, in your view, should be the admission/appointment policy Catholic schools? Why? Can admission policies be adapted to meet specific local situations? What model of Church school underpins your views?

★ Does a school's admission policy affect other schools in the area? In what ways?

[1] LCS 18.  [2] LCS 1.  [3] CS 80;  LCS 16, 17.

When we speak of the ethos of a school we generally refer to the atmosphere or climate which can somehow be sensed within a school community. Ethos is created by means of a great many influences which affect the quality of relationships and the process of learning within the school. Each school has its own distinct environment which is experienced and expressed in such things as the atmosphere of welcome, the visible signs of care, concern and respect for all who make up the school community, as well as the decor, notices and displays. These and other elements of life in school help create a warm, friendly atmosphere or, possibly, the opposite — a cold, distant, even hostile atmosphere. Ethos and the environment that flows from it are **created**, they need to be considered, planned and worked out in practical terms; they do not just happen. The inspiration and challenge for all we attempt to do in this regard are once again our gospel values: the belief that all human beings are uniquely created and loved by God and worthy of respect.

## Relationships

Vatican documents stress that 'before all else, people should find in a Catholic school an atmosphere of sincere respect and friendship'.[1] They insist that the gospel values which we seek to promote are primarily communicated 'through the interpersonal and sincere relationships of its members'.[2] They point out that a 'personal relationship is always a dialogue rather than a monologue' and that we must be convinced that 'the enrichment in the relationship is mutual'.[3]

We need to look at our schools and give serious consideration to the relationships and system of communications which exist between management and staff, between all members of staff at every level of school life — teaching, domestic and administration, between staff and pupils and their families, and between the pupils themselves. We

should ensure that we not only talk about and exhort a spirit of community at assembly and on other occasions, but that we make real efforts to create a community which incorporates all who work, learn and are involved in the school.

## Discipline

There is obviously a need for discipline and order with clear rules and regulations which make this possible. We give greater priority to creative imagination than to dull regularity and an exaggerated sense of order which judges small incidents out of proportion. It is important to create a relaxed environment in which friendly relationships can flourish. We make known the system of sanctions which operates in our schools. If our schools are inspired by the gospel we incorporate into our system forgiveness, healing and reconciliation. We avoid labelling pupils and holding lasting grudges. Pupils should feel that they can redress any wrong they may have done.

## Respect

If we live out our belief that all human beings are uniquely created by God, all staff and pupils will feel accepted and respected. Their gifts and abilities, however we assess them, are to be recognised and developed in 'an atmosphere permeated by the gospel spirit of freedom and love'.[4] There should be no favourites, no marginalised, no outcasts. The sanctions we employ should not rob pupils of their dignity as persons. We seek to help our pupils to have a healthy self-respect

and to be respectful of others. By means of our own open attitude and by encouraging a spirit of cooperation we foster friendship among our pupils which will lead to a mutual understanding and respect for their different cultures and backgrounds.

### Welcome and interest

We aim to make all who come into our schools feel welcome. School secretarial staff play a key role in this regard. It is often difficult for visitors to find their way around schools; frequently there are few notices giving clear directions. Often notices seem more inclined to discourage parents and others from entering the school since they list prohibitions and conditions which may exacerbate the nervousness felt by many parents.

We make particular efforts to help children feel welcome when they first come to our schools — their very first day at school, arriving at a new school, at times of transference from infant to junior, from junior to secondary. For many children these can be bewildering and even traumatic experiences. We try to show and express continuing interest in pupils once they have left the school.

[1] LCS 77.    [2] CS 32.    [3] LCS 33.    [4] DCE 8.

The quality of faith lived in our schools will also be indicated by the way we welcome and treat the poorest and most difficult children and young people.

# QUESTIONS

★ In what ways can schools set about creating an ethos or atmosphere inspired by Christian faith and values?

★ How important do you consider the points stressed in the Vatican documents?

★ If other schools do this, in what respect are Catholic schools distinctive? Does 'distinctive' mean 'totally different'?

★ How important is discipline? Is it possible to be firm and forgiving? What forms of sanctions do you think degrade pupils?

★ Can you describe any notices to visitors which you have seen in schools? What do you think of them? How can schools make pupils, parents, visitors feel welcome?

★ Do you think that a mark of our schools is a readiness to welcome the poorest and care for the most difficult? Should this be a distinguishing mark?

When we speak of the school curriculum we refer very broadly to all the learning experiences which the school provides. Curriculum is an extensive term which encompasses the full network of experiences on which we draw, consciously or unconsciously; it includes the knowledge and experiences to which we expose our pupils, the ways in which we do this and the methods which we employ, as well as the process by which we monitor and evaluate what we do. Ethos and environment are aspects of the school curriculum and are sometimes referred to as 'the hidden curriculum'.

### Our Christian perspective

As Catholics we have a concept of human life and human dignity which is rooted in our belief that Jesus is the revelation of God and the model for our humanity. In planning the curriculum we attend to the physical, intellectual, emotional and spiritual development of all our pupils. While we provide a wide range of learning experiences, we take account of pupils across the wide spectrum of ability. Teachers will bring to each area of learning particular methods and enable pupils to acquire a variety of skills.[1] We recognise the role of the curriculum in developing attitudes, relationships, beliefs, and moral and spiritual values. We do not fragment the human person into neat, distinctive compartments. Our schools do not provide a secular education with a religious appendage. A person is given unity and significance by the spiritual dimension of life. Our curriculum planning has as its foundation this concept of human life.

### Policy and responsibility

The curriculum policy of our schools will take account of the directives put forward by the DES, the LEAs and other responsible and interested bodies. It is, however, the responsibility of our governors, heads and staffs to ensure that curriculum policy is in accord with the aims and Catholic character of our schools.

On occasions we may take up a position of 'critical solidarity' with the educational aims set out by these agencies; at times we may feel obliged to oppose them. This is a task which is all the more delicate and crucial at a time when government is planning radical changes in education, including the introduction of a national curriculum. The implications of this and other policies must be considered in the light of our Christian perspective on educating the whole person within the social, cultural context of our schools. At a time of increased demands and pressure for change we need to be advised, guided and supported by diocesan and national Catholic agencies.

I I could buy clothes for the children in Africe. I would buy then scarves and dresses and knickers to keep them warm at night
Lindsey.

## Special needs

Since the Warnock Report* we are more aware of the special educational needs of children with particular learning difficulties. These difficulties take a variety of forms and arise from a range of causes. We integrate these children into the life of our schools, identify their needs and make suitable and adequate provision for them. This is an important issue and one which cannot be overlooked by schools which seek to live the gospel message.

Our schools — primary, secondary and sixth form colleges — must see that distinctive provision is made for pupils who do not, in one way or another, seem to fit the 'normative' educational models and procedures.

In the production of resources and materials the National Project will consult and take advice from those with experience in this work. It will also invite them to provide guidelines which will help us to fulfil this task in our schools and parishes.

## Multi-cultural education

One of the current priorities of our educational task must be to prepare our pupils for life in a multi-cultural, multi-racial society. Our curriculum must reflect a sympathetic understanding of the different cultures and races in Britain today. This applies equally to all our schools whatever the ethnic mix of the pupils and staff. They must take account of the Swann Report* and of the bishops' report *Learning From Diversity*.

A multicultural perspective should inform the whole of our curriculum; it should not be left to those who teach religious education

[1] CS 39.

and social studies. It should challenge and take positive steps against any racist and ethnocentric mentality: the habit of regarding one's own race or culture as superior to that of others. Racism is not just a matter of personal attitudes. It operates in a more destructive yet more subtle fashion at a structural or institutional level: admission policy, groupings, literature, assessment, for example. In this, as in other curriculum areas, we need assistance and training.

A working party from the Committee for Community Relations of the Bishops' Conference and the Catholic Association for Racial Justice will ensure that all National Project resources reflect this concern. They will also provide practical guidelines for home, school and parish.

## Education for personal relationships

The Church recognises that children learn the art of human relationships first and foremost in the experience of the relationships of the home. It is the responsibility of parents to inform and educate children in all matters which pertain to human growth and development, particularly in the sensitive area of sexual development. The school can and should play a positive part in this aspect of educating the whole person.

The general atmosphere and the relationships which exist in the school help form the attitudes and values of our pupils. While specific members of staff will be responsible for the development

and coordination of programmes, the responsibility must be shared by all the staff. The whole range of the curriculum can help to develop gradually and progressively in our children and young people responsible attitudes in matters concerning personal and sexual relationships. Proper regard should be given to the process of moral development of the young. It is not enough that we inform them of the Church's teaching, we must try to help them appreciate the values embraced in such teaching. Several dioceses have produced guidelines for schools in these matters. It is crucial that parents are informed of and collaborate in this work. Schools should liaise with parish and other groups who specialise in this area and can provide resources.

## Development, justice and peace education

One of the distinctive features of our Catholic schools must be a concern for justice : 'motivated by the Catholic ideal, the Catholic school is particularly sensitive to the call from every part of the world for a more just society, and it tries to make its contribution towards it'.[1] We must see to it that our curriculum reflects this concern.

From our Christian perspective it is an essential aspect of education to make ourselves and our pupils more aware of and sensitive to these issues and ways in which we can take appropriate action. An essential aspect of curriculum is social development which prepares pupils to take their place in society. We encourage them to be socially committed. We seek to enable them to work for more just social structures which give fuller expression to gospel values. In the light of the tremendous problems in the world today — hunger, illiteracy, poor standards of living of many people, violence, abortion etc. — we should cultivate in our pupils a keen social awareness and a profound sense of social and political responsibility.[2]

Schools will find useful resources in the educational publications of CAFOD and Pax Christi. National Project resources to assist in this area are already being prepared — the Just People series for primary and secondary schools.

# QUESTIONS

★ Do you agree that curriculum should address the *whole person* and meet the needs of *all pupils*? Which dimensions of the person should it address? Have you any priorities? How can it meet the needs and abilities of pupils?

★ What are your views on the importance and relevance of provision for
  * special needs?
  * multi-cultural education?
  * education for personal relationships?
  * development, justice and peace education?

★ Are they adequately provided for in your schools?

★ Are there other areas of concern which we have not mentioned?

[1] CS 58.  [2] LCS 18, 19.

# Worship and prayer

Worship as a corporate activity is a feature of most religions. The community celebration of what we believe about God and our life in relationship to God and each other is an essential dimension of our Catholic tradition and is a feature of our schools.

We will mark the liturgical seasons and major feasts. We do this in liturgy and sacrament, in ritual and symbol and in various forms of prayer. In our schools we provide opportunities for such experiences. This is the responsibility of all in the school. The chaplaincy team and the R.E. department in secondary schools may play a coordinating role; they do not carry the entire responsibility.

### Adapted to needs

It is important that we plan and organise these experiences in accordance with sound educational and pastoral principles which are sensitive to the needs of all pupils and staff who take part in them. They must be suited to the age, social and religious development of our pupils[1]. They should incorporate the various cultures which may exist in the school. They must also be sensitive to the perspective and needs of those who belong to other Churches and faith traditions, be respectful of their gifts and enable them to be involved.

Younger pupils will probably take part readily and willingly in acts of worship and prayer; older pupils may express reluctance and resentment if they feel obliged to worship and pray. We must be respectful of their desire for independence and different levels of faith while we seek to enable them to understand and experience the spiritual value of worship and prayer.

### Participation, involvement

In liturgical and other forms of celebration the full and active participation of those who take part 'is the aim to be considered before all else'[2]. This is especially important in celebrating with children[3]. They need to be involved as much as possible in body and mind : through words, song, dance, gesture, music, as well as through silence, reflection, listening and sharing. Celebrations grow out of work which pupils have done in class and are concerned with their lives and experiences[4].

This demands careful preparation. In the occasion of Eucharistic celebration priests, teachers and pupils should, as far as possible, work together in planning and

preparing the liturgy. If priests do not have the time to do this they should at least consult with those who have prepared the celebration so that they do not overlook their work and upset and disappoint the children[5]. It is suggested that if priests find it difficult to get on the wave length of children, the teacher could preach the homily which could involve the children by referring to their work[6].

Celebrations are joyful, community experiences. They should not be presented in too didactic, arid and cerebal a fashion[7]. We must allow and enable our children and the young to celebrate in ways suited to their season of faith.

## Different forms of celebration

All liturgy need not be identified with Eucharist. We recognise the value of other forms of celebration and prayer[8]. These can help our Catholic pupils prepare for and give them a deeper appreciation of the Eucharist and other sacramental celebrations.
There should be celebrations which make it possible for all staff and pupils, whatever their religious allegiance, to plan experiences of worship in which all can participate fully.

Elements of the Eucharist and the worship of other faith traditions provide useful ritual for these : greetings, listening, forgiving and being forgiven. Other basic symbols can provide a focus for worship, celebration and prayer; as can our human hopes and fears. The belief that our lives and the world are sacred because they are created by and destined for God and that God is present with us, makes our experience a foundation for worship, meditation and prayer.

## Assembly

All this applies equally to assemblies. Participation and involvement as well as the creation of a climate of reflection and celebration should be the major concern. Pupils should not passively receive instructions or be invited to join in some prayer formula. The cooperation and coordination of different teachers and classes make it possible to provide a varied form of interesting and inspiring assemblies which arise out of work done and which are a stimulus for further reflection in class.

In many schools, particularly secondary, there are practical problems such as lack of facilities and large numbers. However, we should not be content to hold assemblies which are impersonal and irrelevant. We should avoid a mishmash of administration and religion: notices, rewards and punishments plus a reading, a hymn and prayers. We should set clear goals for our assemblies and assess their value by taking account of the opinions of staff and pupils.

# QUESTIONS

★ In what ways does your school mark the liturgical seasons and special feasts?

★ Should feasts of other faiths be marked — especially those of staff and pupils in the school? How?

★ In what ways can pupils be actively involved in planning and celebrating liturgy and assemblies?

★ Do you think eucharist should be celebrated with the whole school? With small groups? How often? Would you give different answers for primary and secondary pupils? Why?

★ Should such liturgies be voluntary or not? For what reasons?

★ How can sensitivity to those of other traditions be shown?

★ What is the purpose of assembly? How would you achieve it?

[1] DCM 9.   [2] CSL 14.   [3] DCM 22.   [4] DCM 51.   [5] DCM 29.   [6] DCM 24.   [7] DCM 23, 25.   [8] DCM 27.

# Chaplaincy, groups, away-days

Among the distinctive features of our schools is the link with local parishes. Our Catholic communities not only pay money for our schools, they express interest and concern by the presence of priests and others who represent the community of faith. Our schools should welcome and encourage them to play a part in the life of the school. Schools should also work with and be of service to our Catholic parishes in ways which take account of the age, development and interest of pupils. Dioceses and parishes must make our schools a major part of their pastoral concern.

## Chaplaincy

It is the responsibility of the Church community at local and diocesan level to consult with Heads and teachers in order to ensure that there is a pastoral strategy which safeguards this distinctive feature of our schools.

In our secondary schools pupils come from several or many parishes. It is not easy to maintain direct links. For this reason it is important that the community set up some chaplaincy organisation. This task may be shared between a number of people and the coordinator could be a layperson, a religious or a priest. Some aspects of the chaplaincy work will of necessity require the involvement of a priest. However this work is organised, those who do it will liaise and cooperate with priests and parishioners.

The community of school and parish should seek to provide and furnish suitable facilities — chaplain's room, chapel or prayer room, and financially recompense those who do the work. Those appointed should be able to relate well to staff and pupils and should have an appreciation of the educational aims of the school while not being identified with the authority structures of the school. Governors should treat this as a priority in our schools.

## Some tasks

Chaplains serve the personal and spiritual needs of staff and pupils. Their task is pastoral in the broadest sense and demands that they cooperate with other members of staff who hold specific roles within the pastoral care system of the school. They will help coordinate worship, liturgy and prayer with the whole school or with small groups. They will be available as counsellor and friend; will cultivate a trust and openness with members of the school community by being around and chatting with individuals and groups. They can provide comfort and support in times of trouble or crisis especially at times of sickness and bereavement. They can build bridges between school and home. They can encourage pupils to undertake suitable ministries and make it possible for them to exercise these in the school and parish community.

## Voluntary groups

Part of the role of chaplaincy is to foster, encourage and coordinate appropriate catechetical and spiritual experiences for staff and pupils. Groups can be invited to a variety of forms of meditation and prayer. Provision can be made for Catholic staff and pupils to prepare and celebrate the sacraments of Eucharist and Reconciliation.

Challenge and support can be given to groups who come together in order to reflect and act on issues of social concern at home and abroad. Chaplains can promote ecumenical activity and dialogue between staff, pupils and local people of different faith traditions. The value of such voluntary groups in our schools should not be overlooked. They allow children and the young to influence and be influenced by their peers. They provide practical experience of being involved in and organising groups which perform a service to the community.

Members of staff should be encouraged to give time to this work. The support and guidance of interested adults is necessary and allows pupils and staff to cooperate in less formal ways.

There should be links with the Catholic Youth Services, youth workers and other agencies who have a special interest in young people. Pupils can be encouraged to be involved in these and other groups.

## Away-days, retreats

Many teachers are convinced of the great value of away-days and retreats for our younger and older pupils. These give staff and pupils the chance to share in reflection, discussion and prayer in a more personal and community way than is possible in school and classroom.

A number of retreat and conference centres offer pleasant settings and have special programmes which are suited to various age-groups.

Chaplains and teachers often prefer to work out their own programmes or plan sessions with members of staff of these centres. Attendance is often optional; some schools expect all pupils to attend because they consider that the experience is worthwhile for a whole class and helps create a sense of community.

If they are to be of value, they must be carefully prepared, offer a variety of experiences and be sensitive to the age, development and needs of all who take part in them. The experience of friendship, liturgy and prayer on these occasions can leave a lasting impression on the young and arouse a renewed interest in religion. Chaplains and other staff should make sure that there is a useful and balanced follow-up within the school.

The school and local community should provide the necessary support and encouragement for these activities.

# QUESTIONS

★ What links can exist between parishes and primary schools? How can they serve each other?

★ How important do you consider some form of chaplaincy to be in secondary schools and sixth form colleges? Why?

★ What form would you suggest — a priest? Layperson/religious? A team?

★ Do you agree that links with parishes/chaplaincy are a distinctive feature of our schools? Do you think this is given sufficient consideration?

★ What value do you see in away-days/retreats? Should they be optional — always/sometimes?

# Staffing

When appointing staff to our schools we look for people who are highly qualified and competent in their own particular field and who will at the same time contribute to the Catholic character and ethos of the school.

## Competent and cooperative

As a community we encourage suitable Catholics to value and enter the teaching profession and to apply for posts in our schools. It is for this reason that we established and continue to support Catholic Colleges of Higher Education. The number of these colleges has been reduced drastically in the past two decades. We acknowledge the devotion and service given by many members of staff who are not Catholic and we recognise our obligations towards them.

The cooperation of all on the staff in trying to achieve the aims of the school can be a powerful witness and a means of promoting the dialogue and openness called for by the Church after the second Vatican Council. In a context of collaboration and concern for the ideals and values of the school, diversity of religious belief and conviction provides a valuable resource which can be tapped. The gifts of all staff should be valued and they should all feel respected members of the school community.

## Induction

The prospectus and job description should inform all members of staff of our rationale and practice. We cannot simply presume that they have a knowledge of this or that they will gradually pick it up. This applies to young probationary teachers, to those coming from other schools and to those taking up senior posts. It is essential that clear guidelines are available and that the Head and other staff take time to discuss these and their practical implications with new members. They should be made to feel welcome and helped to settle as quickly as possible. This is an element of the ethos we seek to create; it is care for such details which creates it.

## Stress and strain

Heads and teachers in our schools increasingly feel themselves under very considerable stress and strain. This is manifested in the number who opt out of education or take early retirement. It is felt and expressed by dedicated and competent teachers.

In many places amalgamations and the procedure of reapplying for jobs have caused tensions and dissatisfaction. Teachers feel pressurised by falling roles, inadequate resources, poor salary structures. Industrial action has often caused friction in staff rooms. The seemingly endless demands for curriculum change and development can give the feeling of 'initiative fatigue' and bring about a lack of confidence. These and other factors have led to a decline in morale in many teachers.

Despite the difficulties, most have a high regard for their task, value their special relationship with children and the young and the unique contribution they can make to the life of society and the Church.

## Pastoral care of staff

We must be attentive to the needs of teachers and all staff in our schools. Practical structures should be set up which can provide suitable care : the creation of formal and informal support groups for reflection in a relaxed atmosphere, for celebration and prayer relevant to their needs and situation, for social gatherings which are open to all staff.

If we are to create a Christian ethos in the school, we must seek to create among staff an atmosphere of openness and frankness in which differences of opinion can be expressed, respected and conflicts resolved. Staff should be involved in planning and evaluating curriculum and ethos of the school. Whatever our ideals for our schools, we are all fallible and imperfect human beings who make mistakes and fail from time to time. A community which professes to be inspired by the attitude and action of Jesus should see that it provides structures for support, acceptance and forgiveness as well as criticism and challenge.[1]

[1] CS 65-68, 78-80. LCS 15, 73-80.

# QUESTIONS

★ What qualities do you look for in teachers in our Catholic schools? How can they contribute to the creation of the ethos?

★ In what ways can all staff, whatever their task — management, teaching, administration, ancillary etc., contribute?

★ Do job descriptions and prospectus clearly indicate the rationale and expectations of the school? How are staff inducted and made welcome?

★ In what ways can staff be made to feel that they are respected and valued? What structures are there which enable them to express their opinions and play a part in planning and evaluating policy?

★ Do you agree that there is a decline in morale among teachers? What are the causes? How can they be helped? What support structures would you suggest?

★ In what ways can all who are involved in the different aspects of school life feel that they are members of the one staff? Is that important?

# The National Project and our schools

*Living and Sharing our Faith* is the title of the National Project of Catechesis and Religious Education which involves the Catholic community of England and Wales.

The National Project is essentially a community effort. It seeks to use and coordinate the talent and expertise of those in the community who are actually working in the field of catechesis and religious education. It entails a process of consultation, reflection and action which will provide useful and practical resources suitable to the various needs of Catholics of all ages, in different situations and at different stages of their faith journey. Published resources are primarily for use in parish, home and school settings and their publication will extend over a period of years.

## BASIC TEXTS

*Our Faith Story* A.P. Purnell SJ

> The backcloth to the thinking and approach of the National Project. This book is about faith and how it grows and develops. It is about the values which follow from faith and how they affect our lives.

*Guidelines* Jim Gallagher SDB

> *Guidelines* offers an overall picture of the scope and purpose of the National Project. It discusses the national scene, basic principles, the needs of people from children to the elderly and the settings in which we live and share our faith.

## RESOURCES FOR SCHOOLS AND CLASSROOMS

*Our Schools and our Faith* Jim Gallagher SDB

*R.E.: The Primary Years* Danny Sullivan *(in preparation)*

> Practical guidelines which consider the context, content, approaches and resources

of religious education in the primary school.
Other texts will follow from this basic text: e.g. liturgy and assemblies, various themes suitable for nursery and primary children.

*Weaving the Web: A Modular Programme for RE* for secondary schools
Sr Mary McClure SND and Richard Lohan

> Classroom materials for ages 11-14. Modules are provided for 6 themes: People, Community, Story, Values, Communication, Celebration

> Each classroom book will contain 3 modules for one age-band. A Teacher's Book will accompany the pupil's materials.

Just People Series
*Just Seniors* Sr Judith Russi
*September 1988*

> Multi-level, multi-ability resource materials for secondary classes working with justice and peace themes in RE. The pupil's book contains material for 6 themes: Life on

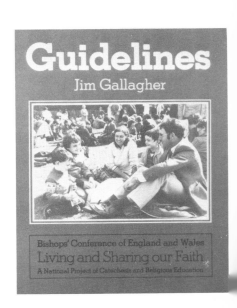

earth; Prophets today and yesterday: changing the system; Women and children: different and equal; Facing injustice and suffering; The point of suffering: victorious victims; Building together: community and peace.

A Teachers Book will accompany the pupil's materials.

Work has begun on *Just Juniors*

## OTHER PROJECT TEXTS

*All is Gift* Guidelines for parish catechists working with children
Lynn Walker SHJM and others

*To Be a People of Hope* Adult Education: a Christian Perspective
A. Patrick Purnell SJ (ed)

## IN PREPARATION

*Parish Approaches*: Guidelines for living and sharing faith in the context of our parishes   A. Patrick Purnell (ed)

*Family Approaches*: reflections on living and sharing faith in the context of our families   Working Group

*Barriers to Community*: Living and sharing our faith in a culturally, racially and religiously diverse society   Working Group

For further information about the National Project, please write to the publishers:
Collins Religious Publications,
8 Grafton Street, London W1X 3LA

# SOURCES AND REFERENCES

**VATICAN II**
*Dogmatic Constitution on the Church* (Lumen Gentium)
*Constitution on Sacred Liturgy*
*Pastoral Constitution on the Church* (Gaudium et Spes)
*Decree on Ecumenism*
*Declaration on Christian Education*
*Declaration on the Relationship of the Church to non-Christian Religions*

**SYNOD DOCUMENTS**
*Evangelisation in the Modern World*, Paul VI, CTS, 1975
*Catechesis in Our Time*, John Paul II, St. Paul Publ., 1979
*Justice in the World*, in *Proclaiming Justice and Peace*, Cafod/Collins, 1984

**VATICAN DOCUMENTS**
*General Catechetical Directory*, S. Congregation for the Clergy, CTS, 1971
*The Catholic School*, S. Congregation for Catholic Education, Catholic Information Office, 1977
*Lay Catholics in Schools: Witnesses to Faith*, S. Congregation for Catholic Education, CTS, 1982
*Educational Guidance in Human Love*, S. Congregation for Catholic Education, CTS, 1983
*Directory on Children's Masses*, S. Congregation of Divine Worship, CTS, 1974

**NATIONAL CHURCH DOCUMENTS/REPORTS**
*Synodal Letter*, 17th July 1852, Bishops of the Province of Westminster, in *The Synods in English*, Guy E. (ed), St. Gregory's Press, Stratford-on-Avon, 1886
*Memorandum on the Appointment of Teachers*, Bishops of England and Wales, Education Commission, 1974
*Memorandum on School Chaplains*, Department of Catechetics, 1979
*The Easter People*, Bishops of England and Wales, St. Paul Publ., 1980
*Signposts and Homecomings: the Educative Task of the Catholic Community*, St. Paul Publ., 1981
*Catholic Education in a Multi-Racial Society*, Catholic Commission for Racial Justice, Briefing, July 2nd, 1982
*Learning From Diversity: A Challenge to Catholic Education*, Report on Catholic Education in a multi-racial, multi-cultural society, Catholic Media Office, 1984
*Religious Education in a Diverse Society* (Discussion Paper), Working Party, Briefing, 1st May 1987
*Evaluating The Distinctive Nature of a Catholic School*, Co-ordinating Committee for In-Service, Evaluation, Appraisal in Catholic Schools, Department of Christian Doctrine and Formation, 1987
*Catholic Schools and the Education Reform Bill*, Bishops of England and Wales, Diocesan School Commissions, 1988

**NATIONAL EDUCATIONAL DOCUMENTS/REPORTS**
*Special Educational Needs, the Report of the Committee of Enquiry into the Education of Handicapped Children and Young People*, Warnock H.M. chairperson, HMSO, 1978
*Meeting Special Educational Needs*, A Brief Guide to the Warnock Report, H.M., HMSO 1978
*The Education Act 1980 and Catholic Schools, Guide to the Act*, Catholic Education Council, 1980
*The Education Act (no. 2) 1986 and Catholic Schools, Guide to the Act*, Catholic Education Council, 1986
*Parental Influence at School* (White Paper), HMSO, 1984
*The Curriculum for 5-16*, DES, HMSO, 1985
*Quality in Schools, Evaluation and Appraisal*, DES, HMSO, 1985
*Education for All*, the Report of the Committee of Enquiry into the Education of Children from Ethnic Minority Groups, Lord Swann chairperson, HMSO, 1985
*Education for All*, A Brief Guide to the Main Issues of the Swann Report, HMSO, 1985
*Better Schools* (White Paper), HMSO, 1985

**NATIONAL PROJECT TEXTS WITH REFERENCES TO SCHOOL**
*Our Faith Story*, A.P. Purnell SJ, Collins 1985
*Guidelines*, Jim Gallagher SDB, Collins, 1986

**BOOKS/ARTICLES**

| | |
|---|---|
| Francis L. | 'Roman Catholic Secondary Schools: falling roles and pupil attitudes', *Educational Studies*, Vol. 12, no. 2, 1986 |
| | 'Are Catholic Schools good for non-Catholics?', *The Tablet*, 15th Feb, 1986 |
| | 'The Choice for Catholic Schools', *The Tablet*, 4th Oct, 1986 |
| Fowler J. | *Stages of Faith*, Harper & Row, 1976 |
| Moran G. | *Religious Education Development*, Winston Press, Minneapolis, 1983 |
| Nichols K. | *Cornerstone*, St. Paul Publ., 1978 |
| Rossiter G. | 'Catechesis and Religious Education: The Need for a Creative Divorce in Catholic Schools,' *Religious Education*, 77, 1, 1982 |
| Rummery R.M. | *Catechesis and Religious Education in a Pluralist Society*, E.J. Dwyer, Sydney, 1975 |
| Rodger A.R. | *Education and Faith in an Open Society*, Handsell Press, 1982 |
| Watson B. | *Education and Belief*, Blackwell, 1987 |
| Westerhoff J.H. | *Will Our Children Have Faith?*, Seabury Press, New York, 1976 |